The Journey Home

THE JOURNEY HOME

A Father's Gift to His Son

CLIFTON L. TAULBERT

Council Oak Books

San Francisco / Tulsa

Council Oak Books, LLC

1615 S. Baltimore Avenue, Ste. 3, Tulsa, OK 74119

THE JOURNEY HOME: *A Father's Gift to His Son.* Copyright © 2002
by Clifton L. Taulbert. All rights reserved.

Designed by Melanie Haage
Photograph on page 6 by Richard Downing © 2002
Other photographs courtesy of Clifton Taulbert's
personal collection © 2002

Library of Congress Cataloging-in-Publication Data to come.

ISBN 1-57178-117-X
First edition / First printing.
Printed in Canada.

02   03   04   05   06   07   5   4   3   2   1

Right away I asked the young man a thousand questions about the Delta. Like so many people away from home, he was eager to tell me all about it, everything he missed: the cool black loam, the cool well water, the cool breeze his mother prayed aloud for before every summer supper.

— From *Charms for the Easy Life* by Kay Gibbons

I am a part of all that I have met.

ALFRED LORD TENNYSON

One

It was fall in Tulsa. The hot, humid air outside had turned mild, and the evenings were cool and sweet. It was the week before Thanksgiving, five weeks before Christmas, and retail America was already preparing for another big holiday season. As always, the stores around town were getting ahead of themselves and decorating for the biggest spending season of the year before we even had a chance to carve the Thanksgiving turkey. Christmas music was piped into every store, decorations sprang up in every shop window, and signs warned us that there were *less than forty shopping days left!* We didn't even have to leave the house to feel the retail spirit. With each day's mail, another stack of glossy catalogs arrived to tempt us with everything from stereo systems to silk bathrobes. The mailbox was so stuffed with commercial reminders of the upcoming holiday, I wondered if there would be room left for the Christmas letters from family and friends that I looked forward to every year.

Both my son and his mother took advantage of this marketing deluge to leave helpful reminders around the house, turning down catalog pages, and marking items with stars and circles. I would find catalogs strategically placed where I was sure to see them and left open to a certain page, drawing my attention to a gift idea that someone felt particularly suited their fancy. If that was not enough, my twenty-year-old son, Marshall, hinted to my wife, Barbara, and me by talking loudly on the phone to his friends, describing how much he was hoping to receive this or that gift.

One evening, Barbara and I sat down in the den to discuss our Christmas plans and what our gift for Marshall would be. A CD burner? An MP3 player? One of those new high-end turntables he was always talking about? The ever-present catalogs crowded around in stacks, vying for our attention. We perused the stereo and electronic equipment, laughing and talking together. There were plenty of items that would be sure to please him.

"He doesn't need any more electronic gadgets," said Barbara. "The upstairs den is a sea of wires and speakers already."

We fell silent, hunting through the catalogs for ideas.

"We could get something for the truck," I suggested. "He liked the off-road tires we got last year." Tires, I thought to myself, that were probably worth more than plenty of people's cars.

"That was last year. This year we should do something

different," said Barbara, flipping past page after page of colorful merchandise arrayed on smiling models. "He doesn't like clothes, and I can't think of anything else he needs."

As we listened to ourselves, we both realized how different Marshall's world is from the world we were raised in. Barbara grew up in rural Arkansas, the third oldest of eleven children, living on her parents' cotton farm. Christmas time was joyfully welcomed, but often brought little or nothing in the way of toys. I grew up in a small town in the Mississippi Delta, where cotton and hard work ruled our lives. There, too, Christmas had been about friends, family, and good food, not lavish gifts. Our son was living as we had once only dreamed of doing. Already in college, he was also on the cusp of independence, and his life was beginning to take him further and further away from what Barbara and I called home.

As we sat and talked, considering all the advantages Marshall enjoyed as well as all that he had experienced within the last couple of years, it became quite clear that our increasingly material society was threatening to drown out the family heritage that his mother and I valued so dearly. Marshall had attended a Final Four basketball game where he was escorted to a sky box with the "big guys." Marshall had been mistaken for a member of a famous rap group. This guy was cashing in, and in a big way. He had spent his high school senior trip in Cancun, Mexico, getting wild with all the college students on break.

(When I was a senior in high school, I had not even heard of Cancun.) Now Barbara was hoping that we wouldn't look up one day and see him on one of those candid MTV Cancun specials. We knew he'd had a good time. In the days after he returned, his friends would come over and immediately run upstairs to see the photographs, pictures that were not shared with us.

Before the trip, he had asked for and received our permission to dreadlock his hair using an elaborate method involving wax. Unfortunately, the sun in Mexico was so hot it melted the wax, undoing his new look. Not to be discouraged, he let his friends help him dye his dark, tightly curled hair — blond. Apparently, this process gave him coming-of-age courage. On returning home, my newly blond son told me that he had seen several sunrises while in Mexico, as if to imply that the curfew back home ought to be lifted. I listened and promptly advised him that the rubber band had stretched liberally to reach as far as Cancun for one week, but was now back to normal, as was his curfew.

Earlier that year, he had gone to New York City with his friend Wendell and Wendell's mother. The boys had probably seen more of New York in their short stay than I had seen in ten years of business visits. He had gone down to the trading floor of the New York Stock Exchange and talked about his future with some of the top stockbrokers in America. Several years earlier, he had landed a silent bit part in the movie based on my first book, *Once Upon a Time*

When We Were Colored, a recollection of my childhood, picking cotton in the segregated Mississippi of the 1950s. He was disappointed with me because, as the writer of the book, I had not negotiated him a long and memorable speaking part. I did the best I could: He got to sit behind the male lead while on their bus ride to school. He followed directions well. He kept his head down, looking in his books, a direction I wish he'd follow in college. Now as Barbara and I sat amidst the catalogs, talking and laughing about our son's adventures in the wider world, we wondered, was there anything left to wrap?

Picturing my son carousing with his friends in Cancun, I remembered Glen Allan, Mississippi. I recalled my life among the people who loved and cared for me as a child. They didn't vacation in Cancun. They were maids and field hands. A sprinkling of them were teachers and church workers. I could not help but recall how, as a young boy growing up in the Mississippi Delta, the gifts of Christmas were shared joy and simple pleasures. Miss Martha Dunn made Christmas bread pudding that everyone on our street could hardly wait to sample, and Miss Florence and her boarder Mr. KC would cook until the smell of smothered chicken — a southern slow-cooked delicacy with gravy — mustard greens, and hot corn bread drifted out of the kitchen window and mingled with the smell of the honeysuckle that grew in front of her white house with the long front porch. At Christmas time, I was welcomed at each house and never missed my turn to taste and tell.

It was the season of good food, but it was also the time of giving, when parents might save up all year to get that one special gift. The present I treasured most was a red bicycle, too tall for me to reach the pedals, but small enough to walk around the neighborhood for all to see. I was overjoyed with that big bike, knowing that it would be shared with family and friends for years. Throughout my childhood, it was our neighborhood "horse," and we would take turns riding it like cowboys, decked out with a fancy holster and twin guns, a gift from another special Christmas.

I was younger than Marshall in those days. I was just a kid with plenty of dreams. However, when I was twenty years old, the same as he, I was in the military, anxiously awaiting orders that could have shipped me off to Vietnam. Christmas was a lonely time for me in 1965. I was unable to go home and be with the family who raised me in Glen Allan, or visit the family who had voluntarily taken me in while I was in St. Louis, where I'd been making my way as a dishwasher. It was the coldest Christmas of my life — a time in which I desperately needed the warmth I remembered emanating from the kitchens and lives in Glen Allan. Instead of the two-gun play set I cherished as a boy, I had been issued a real gun with real bullets, just in case my number came up and Vietnam needed my classification.

While I was proud of my son standing and talking with brokers on the floor of the New York Stock Exchange, I couldn't help feeling that Marshall was missing out on valuable consultations with other important people. I recalled my joy at standing in line with my sisters and brother at our great-grandfather's house to get our Christmas gifts and holiday hugs from Poppa Joe, the big man in our lives. Marshall never knew him and never experienced the giant bear hug that seemed to hold you forever.

It had been many years since we had taken Marshall back to my small Mississippi Delta hometown. He'd been only seven years old the last time he visited Glen Allan. He recalls it as the time of the great fight, when he did battle against swarms of blood-sucking mosquitoes. Marshall is allergic to mosquitoes, and there were plenty of them to go around, leaving big, swollen marks on his skin. Every time we mentioned Glen Allan to him after that, he recoiled and hugged his spotted legs, which for a long time bore the telltale signs of his visit to "the country," as he called my hometown. Now he was just about a man, already in college, and he had never experienced the holidays in the world that had shaped my life.

"Why not take him home?" I suggested to Barbara. She knew I meant Glen Allan. I wanted him to experience, in some fashion, the kind of holiday season I always cherished, even if it might not be exactly the way I remembered. The issue was quickly settled: We would drive home to the Mississippi Delta for the holidays and visit friends and family the same way I had many, many years earlier as a child.

I knew from previous trips that much of what I loved and remembered was changing. Death had taken away many of the people who were the most important to me and whom I would have most wanted Marshall to know. Ma Ponk, for example, would no longer welcome him with wide outstretched arms. He wouldn't be able to walk around the corner as I always had, past Miss Big Dump's house, to visit Aunt Mozella and Poppa. It was important for me to outrun time so that Marshall could at least meet some of the people and see some of the places that hold such prominent positions in my mind and heart. I wanted Marshall to share whatever was left of that world, to have a sense of what it had been. This year, I thought, Christmas would be an opportunity to give Marshall a truly valuable gift: the people who had made the holiday season a very real time of joy for me.

Two

Barbara and I were happy with our decision, but we had to figure out how to get Marshall to come with us. We knew he had his heart set on a road trip to Florida with his friends for Christmas. In Florida, there were bright lights and no mosquitoes. One of Marshall's earliest memories of Glen Allan was how dark it got at night. The silent black nights in tiny Glen Allan could hardly compete with the nightclubs and dance music waiting for him in Miami Beach. Fortunately, I knew that Marshall was at the age when he could be persuaded to change positions if the final outcome was tempting enough. To be blunt, I knew my son could be bribed, if it came to that.

The next day, I sat him down on the couch and looked him in the eyes as I spoke to him. I said, "Marshall, your mom and I have decided that we should all go home for Christmas. This may be the last time you have a chance to see and hug the people who took care of me. You need to

*How simple a thing it seems to me that to know
ourselves as we are, we must know our mothers' names.*

ALICE WALKER

see the old people so that you can have stories for your children of where you came from."

"Glen Allan for Christmas?" said Marshall, as though I had suggested a trip to Mars. "Daddy, you must be kidding. The fellas want me to go with them to Florida. We got it all planned out."

"I know how badly you want to go to Florida," I said, "but think for a moment. Your children will need to hear your stories about the world that gave you life."

"Can't I tell them your stories? I can read it from your books," he said, smiling like a wiseacre. "Now that's a good idea."

We laughed for a minute, but when we were quiet I persisted. "Marshall, as your dad, I tell you, the best gift you can give your future is knowledge about your past."

"Daddy, Glen Allan is not my past, it's *your* past. I don't know hardly any of those people."

"I know you don't know them, which is all the more reason for you to fill in this gap by going home. Things are changing in Glen Allan. They've already changed. I want you to get a taste of what that life was like before it's gone for good."

"If I go, I have to give up my trip to Florida," said Marshall, beginning to negotiate. "What do I get for that?"

"The chance to experience your heritage and please your father," I said.

He rolled his eyes.

"Oh, all right, Marshall, if you go home with us willingly, I'll support your semester break trip."

"You got a deal, Dad, but don't try to weasel out on me." He gave me another one of his looks. "How long are we going to stay?"

"We'll probably stay three or four days."

"Three or four days? Daddy, you know that's too long. Let's do two days."

I sighed and shook my head. "Well, we'll see about that."

Marshall had agreed to forego his trip to Florida with his friends. Now all we had to do was wait until the calendar rolled around to December twenty-third. More than once I sat down in my study and took out the road atlas, tracing the route of our trip. We would set out from Tulsa, pick up Interstate 40 to Little Rock, then take 65 South to Greenville on the Mississippi Delta, a short drive from Glen Allan. Meanwhile, Christmas-tree lots sprang up on empty corners around the city, and the hustle-bustle of gift shopping began. Advertisements jockeyed for our attention from radio, TV, newspapers, and billboards. Downtown, hiphop Christmas tunes mingled with the sacred chime of church bells. I waited impatiently for the drive that would take me back to the people and the way of life I held so dear.

The Christmas season is the one time of year when something special is going on just about everywhere, no matter where you live. Back home in the Mississippi Delta where I grew up and my dreams were shaped, the Christmas holiday season was more than special, it was the best time of year. The cotton crops had been laid by, and most of the field workers were off, taking a much-needed rest from their backbreaking labor. Relationships strained by months of hard work were mended with kindness, and ties of friendship and family grew stronger with each day spent relaxing together. Christmas was a time of rest and renewal, sharing and celebration. Far from hectic, it was the time of year when we could focus on the important people in our lives.

The holiday season in Glen Allan was always preceded by weeks of quilting, canning, hunting, and cooking up special dishes. Once the cotton was in, Daddy Julius and my uncles and cousins would catch up on their hunting. Sometimes, if I begged long enough, I got to go along with them. We would walk out into the woods beyond the cotton fields and hunt ducks, squirrels, and rabbits. No Christmas was considered complete without a main dish of fresh game someone had killed with his own gun. Rabbit stew and squirrel, surrounded by baked sweet potatoes, were an important part of the holiday feast, along with ducks, hens, and choice pieces of pork. There was very little beef, but plenty of pork. Nearly everyone raised hogs, and preparing the meat for use throughout winter was also a fundamental part of the Christmas season. Around Glen Allan in December, the salty hickory smell of pork being cured and smoked was heavy in the air.

Soon pantry shelves would be weighed down with cakes and pies, cooked from scratch and smeared with homemade jellies and icing. My favorite was Ma Pearl's five-layer red jelly cake. No one would be allowed to touch anything until Christmas Eve. Even the men who could usually change the rules in the middle of the game got a swat if they laid a finger on a Christmas pie or cake before the twenty-fourth. Whatever the cook said, it was gospel, to be heard and obeyed by all, no matter how delicious the kitchen smelled.

When I was a little boy, Miss Ida, Daddy Julius's second wife, was slowly winning her way into our hearts with her coconut cake. Not much could beat that coconut cake, unless it was something out of Aunt Willie Mae's kitchen. She had the season down pat. She was the resident chef of Glen Allan, and there was no dessert she could not make. The whole town, myself included, waited on her lemon pound cake to come out of the oven. She sang and stirred and sang some more as she cooked, keeping an eye on the cakes arranged on the sideboard. They were glazed with a thick layer of gooey yellow icing that oozed over the edge of the plate in big, delicious lemon-smelling drips. We knew we couldn't get at the cake, but the drips of icing seemed like fair game. We boys considered that icing nothing less than pure gold, and we would risk getting our hands slapped to sneak a taste.

There wasn't much money in the small cotton communities like Glen Allan, but we looked forward to Christmas with all of our hearts just the same. It was a time of celebrating life and relationships. The adults worked and saved so that the delicious smells of Christmas would be everywhere. There were never many store-bought gifts. We didn't get train sets and play rifles and dollhouses like we saw in the windows of the stores in Greenville, our closest big city. But there were plentiful gifts of fresh oranges, apples, and nuts of all kinds. We were always taught to have a gift of some sort for someone else, but it didn't have to be anything expensive. Our love was just as well expressed with a small bag of pecans as it was with a lavish gift.

Glen Allan was hot most of the year, and our houses were not well-suited to the cold of winter. I remember the silent chill outside of Poppa Joe's house fighting to get in. Poppa Joe and Ma Pearl, the people who raised me, kept the icy winds at bay by plugging holes with old clothes and keeping the wood-burning stove in the front room red hot. The big iron stove fought the cold with a fierce heat, and we would crowd around it, joyful and noisy with conversation. The smiling faces and many good wishes for the New Year reflected the warmth in our hearts.

Nobody bought the tall, perfectly shaped trees to deck out with shiny balls and sparkling icicles that everyone expects now at Christmas. We couldn't afford them. Nobody had wreaths on the front door or life-sized Santas standing out in front of the house. Neighbors didn't compete to see who could string the most elaborate display of Christmas lights on their houses and in their yards. We did have our tree, small as it was, with a sprinkling of shredded silver tinsel to give it that holiday feel. More than the tree or any of the decorations, it was Poppa Joe and Mama Pearl themselves, their very presence, that made this wonderful season ours to treasure. They were the look, feel, and life of the holiday.

During this season, our town's humble homes, mostly two- or three-room shotgun houses and a few slightly bigger places with front and back porches, reverberated with laughter and love, a sweetness that sustained us throughout the year. The people in that little community held on tightly to each other. Their hugs were so big and strong and their laughter so deep and real that we never had a chance to worry about what we might be missing. The grownups gave each other the Christmas joy that they carried in their hearts, and it was a tremendous gift. I remember their voices would ring with excitement and wonder as they pooled funds to purchase little gifts of toys and treats like oranges and apples. And there were times when they would save up for a special present that we could all enjoy; for instance, the big red bike I shared with my brothers and sisters and the scores of cousins who descended on our home for holiday visits.

Sitting in my study, thinking of the Glen Allan of my childhood, I realized that urban life and moments of personal success had altered that picture of what makes Christmas special. I knew that this trip back home was about more than seeing friends and relations from long ago. It was about reclaiming a closeness with my family and making sure my son had some sense of its value.

Three

I could hardly wait for December twenty-first. Marshall had completed his finals for the semester, and the time when we would leave Tulsa and head for the Mississippi Delta was drawing closer each day. At last, the holidays would mean more than shopping and catalogs. As Barbara and I planned and packed, I found myself humming old tunes and daydreaming about all the folks back home who had given me my life. I sang Ruth Brown and Muddy Waters, and hummed hymns like "Search Me, Lord," and "I Know That I've Been Changed." I could hear it all again. In Glen Allan, these songs were as much a part of the spirit of the place as the smell of supper cooking.

Sometimes I would laugh out loud as I passed by the photograph of Aunt Willie Mae that hangs in our front hall, remembering the wonderful times and how she used to squeeze me and make me smile. Pictures of Ma Ponk and Poppa Joe, he with his ever-present pipe, seemed to look out at me with a new sparkle in their eyes, silently

There is a destiny that makes us brothers,
no one goes his way alone; all that we send into
the lives of others, comes back into our own.

EDWIN MARKHAM

approving our trip back home. I wandered around the house preoccupied with daydreams of Glen Allan, of Christmas jelly cakes, pecan pies, and baked sweet potatoes that tasted like warm, delectable syrup.

At last the day came when we loaded up the car and set out. We'd rented a minivan for the eight-hour trip so we would have room to stretch out. Barbara and Marshall were soon engrossed in magazines for the drive, *Southern Living* for her and *Sports Illustrated* for him. I glanced in the rearview mirror. Marshall was sprawled in the back seat, looking comfortable, reading about people and places far removed from the world he would soon see.

I believe I could drive to the Delta blindfolded. The journey from Tulsa to Greenville, Mississippi, and finally Glen Allan hasn't changed much in forty years — down through the raw, flat prairie, going south on the Muskogee Turnpike to Interstate 40, east past Little Rock, then south on 65, straight sailing all the way to Greenville. It had been five years or more since I'd been home, and well over a decade since I'd been in Glen Allan during the holidays.

While driving through rural Oklahoma, I saw small towns and simple houses that reminded me of home. When I saw a sign along the highway for a rustic winery, I interrupted Barbara and Marshall's reading. I had to tell them about Miss Sissey's Christmas cake. It was some cake. It was common knowledge that Miss Sissey, my step-great-grandmother, took to the bottle every once in a while, especially while cooking her famous caramel Christmas cakes. I laughed out loud as I recalled not being able to wait to get to her house to get my big slice of that cake. Now I wondered if it was the cake or the sherry in the cake that made Miss Sissey's concoctions such favorites. Both Barbara and Marshall smiled tolerantly. They'd heard this story before, I knew, but, for me, it was as if it had all happened just yesterday.

"Daddy, you really are enjoying this long, tiring trip," Marshall piped up from the back seat, shaking his head and yawning.

"Marshall, do you want to take a turn at driving?" I asked. He was right about one thing. It was a long trip.

"Can't. I left my license at home." He stretched out in the back seat, looking like he might take a nap.

I glanced at Barbara. She'd pulled another copy of *Southern Living* from a stack she'd brought for the ride and was reading recipes. For years, Barbara has indulged my passion for telling stories about my childhood. She will listen and laugh, but they never quite mean to her what they mean to me. How could they?

Barbara is from Arkansas, right across the river from where I grew up, but she had never heard of Glen Allan until we met. Many of the same threads run through our lives, and we share memories of growing up close to the land, places steeped in the rural culture of the South. Barbara was a quiet little girl, raised on a cotton farm. Like me, she remembers Christmases founded on special once-a-year meals and sweets prepared with loving hands, rather than on lavish gifts and fancy toys.

I drove south through Pine Bluff, Arkansas, and finally to Lake Village, where I could almost hear the Delta calling. Lake Village was one of the few places I remember going on a family outing when I was a child. My family would make the trip out to watch the Fourth of July fireworks. It was always a good trip, except for crossing the old bridge, the biggest structure that a little boy from Glen Allan had ever seen. Crossing the long narrow bridge, suspended in midair across the mighty Mississippi River, always made me tense up. I'd look down at the fearsome suck and ripple of the green-brown water rushing and swirling beneath us.

When I saw the worn wood and peeling paint of an old place called the Catfish and Steak House in the bend of Highway 65, I knew that the Mississippi River bridge was coming up. I was right; I was always right. The bridge, a half century older now, rose into view dead ahead. I mustered up my courage, silently saying a prayer for our safety, and drove on.

I was determined that my son would not detect my lifelong fear of that bridge. All those years living in awe of the river had left their mark on me. It just didn't feel right to drive our minivan up and over it, suspended above that ravenous current, as if inviting it to rise up and carry us away. Now I imagined that the bridge was laughing at me, daring me to conquer it one more time. I felt the old fear, felt my palms grow moist and my breath short, but nothing would stop me from giving my son his Christmas gift

— certainly not the old bridge, as formidable as it still seemed. With fingers clinched around the steering wheel and eyes focused straight ahead, I drove across the bridge, all the while racking my brain for options. I thought, there must be a better way to come home.

Soon we landed on the other side, where a strip of concrete road connected the bridge to solid ground. Up ahead, I was delighted to see the skeleton of the old cotton gin that had been standing my whole life, and the decaying general store that I remembered from childhood. They had been my markers for years, signifying that I had passed from Arkansas into Mississippi. I was home.

The cotton fields were still there, looking just the same as I remembered. To the south, I saw the old houses where the "independent blacks" — farmers who had their own places — had lived when I was a child. They were white frame houses with yards and trees and plenty of acres in the back for planting cotton. I'd had a friend in high school, Frank Johnson, who'd grown up in one. He'd seemed marvelously privileged. Very seldom was there a shotgun house in this setting. These farmers were associated with the rural agriculture programs that helped them improve their harvests and get subsidies. They were not tenants, they were landowners. I always felt good when I passed their places.

Up ahead, the old "Welcome to Mississippi" sign beckoned. The type had been changed and the population figures updated, but the painted magnolias around the edges looked the same. Someone had added a small Christmas wreath.

"We are in Mississippi!" I yelled to my dozing wife and son. "We are home."

"*You* are home," said Marshall.

He never misses a chance to remind me that Tulsa, Oklahoma, is his home. He was born at Tulsa's Saint Francis Hospital, duly weighed, foot-printed and stamped into official existence, not delivered by a midwife as I was. Her handwriting on my birth certificate is hard to read, the script of a woman poorly educated in reading and writing, or perhaps a sign of fatigue after a long delivery.

We reached Greenville, Mississippi, our first stop. Greenville was the big city when I was a kid. A trip to Greenville was a special occasion full of wonders, like the big department store and my Greenville relations, whose lives seemed the summit of sophistication compared to anything in Glen Allan.

Dusk was settling in, and the air was brisk. We would relax and get a good night's sleep here in Greenville. The next day, we would visit a few friends and relatives I still knew in town before we went on to Glen Allan. I wanted this to be a time to reconnect with the elders in my life, many of whom had stayed in Greenville. Marshall hadn't met most of these people or had only seen them when he was a little boy. I wanted Marshall, the young man, to have a chance to meet them — the people who had set me on the right track so long ago.

"Dad, you gonna take forever?" asked Marshall, staring at me.

I'd been standing by the car, daydreaming as I watched the evening light change. I hefted my bag and Barbara's out of the back of the rental and headed into the lobby of the Greenville Inn. It had been a long trip, and Marshall was ready to go to bed. Until we checked in, I was controlling his time.

Inside, we were greeted by a woman at the registration desk who looked like a face from Glen Allan. She offered us a tray of holiday cookies still warm from the oven. She was as friendly as I remembered just about everyone in this part of the country to be. She must have noticed how tired and hungry we were because she insisted that we take some of the freshly baked cookies to our room.

Like any Southerner worth her salt, she insisted we "eat up." I laughed. This welcoming phrase brought back a flood of memories. How many times had I heard that in my childhood? I remembered ladies like Miss Sarah Fields and Miss Hester on my street inviting us kids inside to "eat up" and get on our way. I could hear Miss Hester handing out slices of cake, saying, "You boys eat up, now."

There was no question about it, we were home. With warm cookies in hand, it was feeling more and more like Christmas.

Later, getting ready for bed, I thought about the next day and the people we would see. I remembered Cousin Pearl especially. Pearl was my mother's cousin and closest friend. They talked and acted so much alike, they were often taken for sisters, even though Pearl was as light-skinned as my mother was dark. Thinking of her reminded me of her mother, Aunt Fannie. Aunt Fannie and Cousin Pearl were our city cousins, and when we came to Greenville, we were always warmly welcomed into their home.

*Sometimes our light goes out but is blown into flame
by another human being. Each of us owes deepest
thanks to those who have rekindled this light.*

ALBERT SCHWEITZER

Four

The next morning we ate a quick breakfast downtown and headed for Cousin Pearl's. I hadn't been there in years, but I knew I could find my way to Dent Street in Greenville's South End by memory. Plenty of our "colored" friends and family had lived in that part of town. Cousin Pearl still lived in the same small wood-frame house with a narrow porch just big enough for one chair.

As a kid, I'd loved coming up to Greenville at Christmas time to visit Cousin Pearl and Aunt Fannie and catch up on all the family news. Back then, the drive was as much fun as the visit. I remember Mother and our daddy stuffing us kids in the station wagon where we rode with our faces pressed to the windows, taking in the sights. Just about anything — an enormous elm, a new Cadillac, a man selling hats by the side of the road — was like nothing we'd ever seen in tiny Glen Allan. On the way to Dent Street, we would pass beautiful homes with manicured lawns (although even in the city they let their lawns turn brown for the winter). We marveled at the houses strung with hundreds of lights and decorated Christmas trees standing at attention in living rooms and front yards.

We took in all we saw, but our hearts were focused on seeing Aunt Fannie and Uncle Leonard. Aunt Fannie would always be standing there on the front porch, ample on her feet and wearing her long dress and apron, waiting to welcome us in from the cold. Pearl, her daughter, would be there, too, with her big smile and her arms wide and welcoming. We made no exchange of gifts, and the decorations in the house were sparse at best, but we would be lavished with hugs, plenty of good food, and the fond words, "Now stand back and let me take a look at you."

"Are you sure you're going the right way?" Marshall asked from the back seat as he flipped through yet another magazine.

"You wanna drive? You can, you know."

"Hey, I can't drive. Remember, I left my license at home."

I didn't want to wonder if Marshall would enjoy the day. Back in my childhood, being there was a wonderful treat. I could only hope something of what I remembered about this place would still be there and would somehow sink in. True, much of it was gone. Aunt Fannie died many years ago, so I knew Marshall would never experience her warm, welcoming smile or the delicious food she always had ready for company.

After a few false turns down streets with faded signs, at

last we found Dent Street. Suddenly I felt at home. I recognized everything, but all the houses seemed smaller. I
slowed down at the house that used to be Aunt Fannie's
and pointed. "Hey, son, this is where your great-great-
Aunt Fannie lived. I came here every Christmas."

The house appeared to have shrunk, and the tall concrete steps were gone. How could I show Marshall the
house I was seeing in my memory? The excitement of pil-
ing out of the car with my family and running up the tall
steps into her waiting arms and welcoming kisses was
Christmas for me. "Eat up, y'all. There's plenty here,"
Aunt Fannie would tell us as she ushered us into her
kitchen, where our younger cousins Larry and Billy were
already eating at the big round table that took up most of
the space.

Three doors down was Pearl's house, just where it had
always been. There were no cars out front, and the house
looked rather desolate.

"Maybe she's gone to visit her children," Barbara said,
as she strained to see some sign of life behind the thick
curtains.

I got out of the car, walked to the door, and knocked
as loudly as I could. There was no answer. Pearl just *had* to
be home. She was always home during the holidays. There
were no signs of Christmas to be seen; no wreath hung on
her door, no colorful lights blinked around the windows.
No sound answered my knock except the shush of cars on
the next street over. Barbara beckoned for me to come

back to the minivan. I stepped off the porch, then I turned back one more time and listened closely. Now I heard movement behind the door. Pearl was home.

The door opened, and there she stood, her head wrapped to keep out the cold, holding her bathrobe tightly shut as she peered closely at me. She was old now, close to my mother's age, in her mid-seventies. Mother had moved to Tulsa to be closer to me and my sisters and brothers some years earlier. Though Mother's health was not good, she always perked up when we mentioned the Delta and insisted that we visit her Cousin Pearl. Pearl's face broke into the wide smile I remembered so well as she recognized me. I looked back and waved to Barbara and Marshall to get out of the car and join me. Pearl's step was heavy, but her eyes said, "Welcome. Come on in." She was alone now. Her husband had died, and her children were grown.

The air in the front room was hot and close, warmed by the flames of an open-faced gas heater. Pearl didn't seem to hear very well anymore, but she was still an enthusiastic conversationalist. I pulled my chair up close to her and looked into her face as we talked about the family, her children, my mother, and those of Pearl's brothers and sisters who were still living.

Meanwhile, Barbara and Marshall sat quietly. There were no decorations on the walls to trumpet the season, only the call and response of our conversation in a small room on Dent Street. But Marshall was watching. Was

Christmas about passionate conversation? Pearl stopped a moment and turned to him. She looked Marshall over "real good" from head to toe and finally said, "Cliff, he's a fine-looking boy. You in school, I suppose?"

Marshall was caught off guard, but he answered quickly. "Yes'm. This is my first year in college."

She didn't ask him anything else. She nodded. "That's good." Then she turned around and faced the open gas heater, pulling her green terry cloth robe more tightly, focused once again on her private world. Time had slowed Cousin Pearl, but I was glad she was still here, and grateful for the opportunity to sit again in her presence and recall those important gifts of welcome and caring that she had given me for so many years.

From the car, as we were leaving, Pearl's little house, tucked behind the old cinder-block sanctified church, looked even smaller and more desolate. As we drove away, I glanced back at Marshall, who was sitting quietly in the back seat.

"Marshall, when I was a child, many times my Christmas present consisted of just one big, caring hug from that woman." I wanted my son to understand that Pearl's bright gift of the morning's unselfish conversation was still the best kind of giving. He listened but said nothing, lying back on the seat with his eyes partly closed, engrossed in his music.

I drove on. The midmorning winter light took the shine off of everything and the houses looked shabby and dull. Or maybe that's just what I worried Marshall was seeing. To me, it was all beautiful. Soon we were close to where I remembered Cousin Elmer "Caesar" Thompson's house was, not far from the South End. I hadn't been to see him and his wife, Cousin Everlena, for many years and we were long overdue for a visit. While hunting for the exact street, I told Marshall and Barbara about Cousin Caesar's big screened-in front porch, the really big ditch out front with the long narrow bridge, and how my every crossing of that bridge brought a chilling fear of falling. I knew exactly how everything should look.

"Daddy, where are we going? Did you call these people? You just can't go barging in people's homes without calling first," said Marshall.

"Your father can," Barbara said, as she looked at me and shook her head.

When I was a boy growing up in Glen Allan, we had no telephones to use to call in advance, but it didn't matter. We were always expected and welcomed. The people we visited were the same people we had seen and talked with all through the year, but they took on a special way of living during the holiday season. The smell of liniment was banished and conversations about sicknesses were put aside. No aches and pains were discussed at Christmas, this time of hugs and kisses and feasting. Family was expected to visit often, and heavenly cooking smells drifted from every kitchen. Remembering all that, I wanted to get out of the car and run and knock on every door I saw, wishing everyone a Merry Christmas. I wanted to grab my son by the heart and drag him up and down the street to see the people whom I wanted to be standing on their front porches, beckoning us to come in, or else relaxing in front of their fireplaces, taking in the serenity of the season.

Weaving my way down streets that had grown much narrower than I remembered, I almost missed Cousin Caesar's house. I was looking for a big ditch, a narrow bridge, and a long porch that covered the entire front of the house. Finally, I saw a small house with an even smaller screened porch and a wooden plank that stretched across a narrow ditch. The house faced west, and there was a torn tarp tacked up to the roof. I imagined it was used in the summer to ward off the intense southern heat. Green shutters sagged with age, and paint peeled delicately away from the siding. "This can't be the house," I said to myself, yet there was something familiar about it. The entire street was quiet and empty, and not a single Christmas decoration welcomed the season.

Our deepest fear is not that we're inadequate.
Our deepest fear is that we are powerful beyond measure.
It is our light not our darkness that most frightens us . . . we are
born to make manifest the glory of God that's within us.

NELSON MANDELA

five

I was determined to find out if this small house was the great big house I remembered. Barbara and Marshall sat quietly in the minivan, shaking their heads, while I walked across the wooden plank to the front porch, where I looked closely for a name on the mailbox or something definite I could recognize. I didn't see anything, but I still felt drawn to the house. There was only one way to find out if I was right.

I knocked gently, as if not to wake anyone up. After a few minutes, I thought I heard soft footsteps coming to the door. I waited, hoping to see the tall, vigorous cousin I had known as a child. Cousin Caesar had a unique way of talking very quietly, almost without moving his mouth, but he always sported the best Chicago smile in the Delta, meaning broad, confident, and full of big city style. I waited for what seemed like hours. Finally, the door opened, revealing a short and slight man dressed in khaki pants and a plaid woolen shirt. It was Caesar. As I reached out to take his hands, all I could think about were the days when my mother would let me come to Greenville and spend the night. Caesar was a good looker back then, the sort of guy who talked like he'd been everywhere there was to be. He always smoked a big cigar, which, at the time, was a sign of having something — a kind of status symbol, like wearing a gold watch today. His cars were always new, and there was never any dust on his shoes. He was truly our city cousin, always smiling. The fact that he seemed especially proud of being my mother's cousin endeared me to him all the more.

I could tell he recognized me. I took Caesar's hands in mine and gave him a warm hello. Gradually, he straightened up to get a good look at me. It was my tall cousin after all. Time had bent his back and slowed his every movement, but his smile, the one from 55th Street in Chicago, was exactly the same.

We hugged, stood back, and hugged again. The front porch may not have been nearly so big as I remembered, and the ditch was hardly there at all, but his embrace and his smile were unchanged. That smile and the twinkle in his well-worn eyes were all the Christmas presents I could ask for. Barbara and Marshall came up to join me, and we made our way into the cozy front room, where wood paneling stained a rich shade of auburn had always seemed to me a reflection of Caesar and Everlena's good living.

Cousin Caesar was slow and careful while walking back to his chair. Age and illness had diminished the vigor

I remembered, but Caesar and Everlena's generosity was unmistakably the same. As I expected, Cousin Everlena made a big fuss over us. She was still the uptown hostess she had always been, even if she had to move more slowly. And she still loved Caesar. I laughed to myself as I remembered how she used to fuss over him. They were like lovebirds. Both were great church workers and seemed content to spend the majority of their lives serving the church.

Even though I was just a little boy, Cousin Everlena treated me like an honored guest in her home, welcoming me to the best of everything they had to offer. When I came to visit here, I always got to eat in the dining room. I love being fussed over, so I was delighted to see that Cousin Everlena had not changed in that respect. She was still fussing over her Caesar and his family. Like Caesar, she had been ill, but she was still fussing and taking care of her man. I listened as she brought us up to date on the sickness that had come their way and how their close family members had come to their rescue. She apologized for not having cooked for Christmas, but there was no need to do that. I still had plenty of memories of her delicious cooking, memories enough to wrap for Marshall and Barbara.

I could not help but notice how Caesar and Everlina's eyes and faces lit up, just because I had not forgotten them. This was what I wanted Marshall to experience — these dear people and how much joy can flow from just being in their presence.

While we sat talking and catching up, smiling and remembering old times, I waited to hear the words that said it all. Back home, we use the words, "sho looks fine" to cover a strategic analysis of just about anything. It is the endorsement used to approve everything from a grandchild to a pecan pie. I was not disappointed. Cousin Everlena must have been reading my mind as she stood up and looked my Marshall over from top to toe.

"Your boy sho looks fine," said Everlena, nodding her satisfaction. "Looks just like you and his mama, too. Are you in college yet?"

I smiled with pride. "Fine" means so much more when someone like Everlena uses it. She'd made a general assessment of Marshall, and with that one word given her approval. It covered his manners, how his handshake felt, how he'd responded to her questions. With lightning speed, she had sounded his character and was ready to give her verdict. Though years had passed and so much had changed, this time-honored southern ritual had stayed the same. I was rather taken aback by my feelings about it. I knew that it had meant so much to my great-aunt to hear her peers say, "Your boy sho looks fine." It was a verbal certificate of achievement. It validated her efforts and said to the world that she had done a good job rearing me.

I was surprised at how much I had wanted to hear it again, only this time for Marshall, as a validation that I had not forgotten the traditions of my world in raising my son. Cousin Everlena was the expert, and I needed to hear her opinion. Could Marshall feel the importance of that simple statement? Would he know that he must make sure someday to raise his own children to hear the same?

Caesar and Everlena questioned my son about college and his goals, smiling and nodding, then went on to tell us about other young relatives, pointing out new graduation pictures of which they were obviously very proud. Cousin Everlena, hair gray and pulled to the top of her head, talked with pride about cousins I should have known, but had never met. We listened, though, and soon became part of her story. I knew that Marshall's name would become part of their conversations with other family and friends, added to the long list of cousins living away from home, but doing good things. After all, Marshall was their Aunt Pearl's great-great-grandson, and that counted for much.

We sat close together, feeling the warmth and comfort of family, and our conversation took us from one big city to another. Cousin Everlena told us about her granddaughter who had finished college and was off teaching school.

"You know when Caesar took sick, she wanted to come and stay, but I told her we could tough it out, and we did. But she was ready to do whatsoever it took to help us."

I had never met this cousin, but her portrait was prominently displayed along with others I had only heard about.

"Cliff, you spend time out West in California, don't you?" asked Everlena.

"Yes'm," I replied.

"You should look up your cousins out there. Caesar's daughter's children are all out there and doing quite well."

I asked for the address and hopefully, I'll one day get the chance to meet these cousins whose grandparents have meant so much to me. In just a few minutes, we'd found out who was in college, who lived where, who had done well in Los Angeles, who was moving to Dallas. They were weaving accomplishments and expectations, and now Marshall was being woven into the fabric.

Christmas visits were always a time to check in and give an account of your life. Being with Caesar and Everlena brought a flood of childhood memories. Back then, the season of cheer was served up with jelly cake, piping hot coffee for the adults, and a thorough account of the year's accomplishments. I remember smiles and pats to bolster our feelings about ourselves, and to send us off to do better. Sitting here with them now, I saw that some things had not changed. Although we didn't have thick slices of red jelly cake, all the caring looks and deep questioning felt the same. It showed their acute interest in the struggles and successes of each member of their extended family. What I'd most hoped for was coming true: They were teaching Marshall that he was part of something, that people who loved him were watching and hoping he would do well. What we felt and experienced in Caesar and Everlena's front room was of great value, rivaling the experience my son gained from having visited the floor of the New York Stock Exchange.

Cousin Everlena brought out more pictures, and there was more conversation. All the while, Cousin Caesar sat in his comfortable chair taking in the family. Sometimes, we just looked and said very little. After all, it had been years since we had seen each other. I was especially happy when Caesar focused his attention on Marshall. I loved watching my son fumble for answers to questions that had nothing to do with sports, girls, or his travels. Marshall looked at me, and I slowly looked away from him as if to talk with Cousin Everlena. I wanted him to face Caesar as I had done so many years ago and answer the questions himself. I watched out of the corner of my eye as Marshall leaned into the conversation and talked to our cousin as if he had known him all his life.

We were about to leave when there was a knock on the door. Cousin Everlena went to answer it and let out a big holiday, "God bless you!" Two deacons had come from their church to bring their Christmas presents. Both Caesar and Everlena were housebound, but their good church record had not gone unnoticed. Everlena ushered them in, and after all the introductions, the new guests sat down and we listened as they talked about church, asked us questions about our travels and our faith, and just held a good southern conversation. All of a sudden, one of the deacons stood up.

"Brother Caesar, we want to give you and your wife your sacrament 'fore we leave."

I couldn't believe my ears. I had not seen this done for forty years, although it had been a common practice when I was a little boy in Glen Allan. I was glad to see that good living still demanded making house calls. Back then, the local preachers would always make sure that the sick and elderly were provided the necessary elements of their faith. I remembered long ago going with Poppa, who was a local minister with five churches under his pastorate, to various homes to deliver the sacraments of the church — something Marshall had never witnessed.

The deacons produced a worn black box containing the elements of the sacrament and meticulously laid each out as if in the presence of royalty. When all the elements were assembled and properly displayed, they began to sing an old Dr. Watts tune, one that hurled me back to the St. Mark's Missionary Baptist Church where I grew up and where hymn singing was a way of life. As the older deacon led out the song, "Father, I stretch my hands to thee, no other help I know," I felt as if we were all in the presence of the very strength that sustains our families. While he sang and we joined in, I recalled how our mothers and fathers, grandmothers, and grandfathers would lead out with those same soul-stirring hymns. They didn't need any musical accompaniment. They would sing until their worried and worn faces were framed with a hope that would see them through the rigors of a time when segregation defined and overshadowed their every action.

I glanced over at my son and was pleased to see that he was taking it all in. He looked like he wasn't quite sure what was going on, but recognized it as good. As the hymn ended, one deacon motioned for us to stand and hold hands while the other bowed his head and put his hands together in prayer, "going to the Throne of Grace," as they say in the South. While holding my family's hands, I could not help but open my eyes and look around me. Everlena, with her crown of white hair, had her teary-eyed face lifted up in adoration, seemingly unaware of our presence. I watched for a moment as she released her clenched hands from her husband's and Barbara's and awkwardly fumbled at her well-traveled apron, lifting it to catch the tears that slid softly down her cheeks. After wiping away the tears, she grabbed their hands again, completing the circle of faith once more. Beside her, Caesar stood with his head firmly bowed as if looking deep into the earth. For the seven of us, his home had become our temple. I cast a quick, stealthy look at Marshall. He'd been invited into the world of my memory and now was being included in rituals that had sustained my people through many difficult times. These were rituals I had not seen in many, many years. Marshall's eyes were closed tightly, and he held his mother's and my hands as we all became part of the deacons' prayer for the holiday season.

In that modest room, the older deacon prayed as if the holy congregation of the righteous was present. I held

Marshall's hand tightly until the small tray with the elements of the sacrament was passed to each of us. Caesar and Everlena stood with dignified grace as this sacred act of the church was carried out in their home. I watched while they took the elements to themselves, finishing with a resounding "amen," as did the rest of us in our turn.

It was time to leave. As always, we promised not to stay away so long next time and wished everyone a happy New Year. Outside, we pulled our coats tightly around us against the chill air. My heart was warm with love and fond memories as we waved goodbye. In the car, Marshall made sure to rib me about the precarious foot bridge that turned out to be a lowly plank. Satisfied with having performed his duty, he settled back to enjoy the ride.

"Where to next?" he asked, as we slowly drove away. "You are really liking this, ain't you, Dad?"

Six

*F*amily members weren't the only people I wanted to visit in Greenville. These days in Tulsa, we don't visit school teachers like they're icons or oracles, but back home in Mississippi we did. Teachers were important when I was a child. They were more than the people who instructed us at school; they were part of the motivational team that provided the children of Glen Allan with guidance and encouragement that stayed with us throughout our lives. They demanded our attention, and they gave us their love. Visiting our teachers during the holidays was just like visiting family.

I wanted Marshall to meet Miss Jackson, my science teacher, who, like many of her peers, became a permanent part of her pupils' lives. She is a memorable lady and a great educator who has been a lifelong friend to those of us who came from the small cotton communities near Greenville. Miss Jackson expected great things from each one of us. I wanted Marshall to know such a person.

Let us be grateful to people who make us happy;
they are the charming gardeners who make our souls blossom.

MARCEL PROUST

It didn't take us long to reach her place. She still lived on Delta Street off Alexander, in the heart of Greenville's African-American community. As we turned the corner, I recognized the green siding and the carport with the boat trailer off to the side. After all these years, her house hadn't changed at all. From the back seat, Marshall piped up.

"Are you sure she's at home?"

I refused to entertain the thought that she might not be home. "Look at all those cars parked in the driveway," I said. "Can't you tell someone is home?"

Even though I was a grown man with my own family, with both college and post-graduate work to my credit, I still felt a twinge of nervousness as we pulled up. I knew that when I walked into Miss Jackson's house, I would be expected to give an account of myself, as would Marshall. Would my speech be right? Was I dressed okay? Was there anything amiss in my general presentation? Though decades had passed since I'd sat in Miss Jackson's classroom at O'Bannon High School, I still didn't want to disappoint her. I had always relished her approval, and I still wanted her to be proud of me. That was part of what I wanted for Marshall, too. I wanted him to have people in his life who would be part of his dreaming and becoming. We didn't have that in Tulsa, and I felt lucky that I knew where I could still find it.

We rang the kitchen doorbell and waited, exhaling puffs of steam in the cold southern air. Finally, someone came to the door — Miss Jackson's husband, Mr. Jake. He was a retired postman, an enviable position for an African-American in his day. I helped him to remember me, and, happily, he did. He was going out, but called back for his wife to come to the kitchen door.

Soon I saw another face that I had not seen in decades. It was Miss Jackson's sister, who was visiting from California. We were delighted to see each other, and she was equally glad to meet my family. Hustled in out of the cold and standing in the warmth of the comfortable kitchen, we chatted as we waited for my former teacher to join us. It wasn't long until Miss Jackson entered the room like a burst of sunshine, her face lit up with its ever-present glow. She smiled her big smile and opened her arms to welcome us as she had always done.

After she took our coats and caps, she just stood for a minute or two, studying us. In that short time, I realized that nothing that mattered had changed since I was a kid in high school. As she looked us over from head to toe, she began asking questions. "How long are you planning to stay this visit? Now, how are the girls?" Miss Jackson had also taught my two older sisters, and true to her character, she wanted an update on all of us. I tried to answer each question, but often another one popped up before I was finished. Questioning, talking, and keeping her hands moving with enthusiastic gestures, she led us into the living room, a cozy space filled with photographs of her family. There were plenty of places to sit, but we all sat close together, almost touching.

Miss Jackson was in awe of Marshall. He had been just a little boy when she had last seen him, only seven or eight years old. Now he was a tall college student with hair on his face. After hearing about our life as a family, she immediately began to question Marshall about his schooling, grades, and plans for his life.

"Now, young man, and you are the handsome one, what are you majoring in?"

Marshall was quick to answer. "Marketing."

"Have you made plans for graduate school yet?" That question caught Marshall by surprise.

"Well, I'm focused on getting out of college right now."

Miss Jackson nodded. She seemed to be mulling over Marshall's future. "Clifton," she said, "you and Barbara have done a fine job in bringing up your son. I know we'll be proud of his accomplishments."

I am sure that Marshall thought that she was through asking questions, having pronounced her judgment on his upbringing. Not so. She wanted to know his first semester grades. Fortunately, Marshall had done well his first semester. Miss Jackson was delighted and gave him that look of hers, the one that I had always worked so hard to see and enjoyed so much when I saw it. Then she patted his knee, turned to us, and said in a matter-of-fact tone, "I expected nothing less."

Although she had long since retired from the public school system, she was still intent on showing young people that their dreams could come true, and that it was their responsibility to make this happen. I recalled being afraid when I entered ninth grade and had to go up to the big high school in Greenville, but she immediately took charge of my fears and threw them out. Her door was always open. She was willing to take the time to explain the answers to my questions about science and biology.

I remember the first time she called me "Taulbert." I was just "Cliff" back home in Glen Allan, and I thought that being called by my last name gave me a new seriousness and maturity. In Miss Jackson's class, I wasn't just Cliff from little Glen Allan anymore. She treated me like I was from the city and had the same skills as the city kids. She always expected me to excel. She'd say, "Taulbert, you can master this. Just take your time."

Sitting in her living room so many years later, I felt grateful all over again for knowing her, and I hoped that all her students realized how fortunate they were. Miss Jackson also volunteered at her church, teaching bible studies to the kids. She approached that role with the same dedication that she had given to her high school students throughout her career. Now a whole new generation of boys and girls were benefiting from her inspiring words and warm smile. That smile went deep into our hearts and stayed there, telling us that we were alright in spite of what others might say. I needed that when I was in her classes almost thirty years ago, and the confidence she gave me has stayed with me for a lifetime.

I watched my son closely. There in Miss Jackson's living room he was surrounded by photographs of her family, each at a different stage of life, all making her proud in one way or another. She looked at each of her children's pictures and her pride in them came through in every word she spoke. I learned that her son, Jake Jr., was living in Virginia and doing quite well. She told us that her oldest daughter was retiring from the Michigan school system. Her children had excelled in education, medicine, and law, and she seemed to warm at the thought of their prosperity. Her smile grew brighter still as she touched the pictures of her grandchildren, an obvious source of joy. This was what I had wanted Marshall to see and take part in: a world where family was discussed with a proud passion. I wanted him to know a world where "kin" extended far beyond your own front porch and blood relations.

While we sat in the living room talking about the challenges and opportunities facing young kids today, Miss Jackson's sister came and went half a dozen times. Although she was an integral part of the conversation, she also kept getting up and leaving the room, only to reappear a few minutes later. Soon the reason became evident. Each time she left, the door to the kitchen would open. After a while, every time she opened the door, the tantalizing smoky smell of southern cooking would drift into the living room. Without so much as a telephone call to announce our arrival, let alone a formal invitation to visit, we were nonetheless to be treated to a delicious home-cooked meal prepared from whatever was at hand. We would eat lunch with them, that was understood. In that house, there was always something good to eat, and guests were always invited to share it. It was part of who they were.

I can hardly imagine anything to compare with the savory smells and succulent flavors of southern caring wrapped up in the form of collard greens, hot corn bread, macaroni and cheese, leftover roast beef, rice cooked grain-to-grain, and homemade lemonade. There is simply nothing better. After a prayer offered by Miss Jackson's sister, we sat down to celebrate the season with good food and friends. Our conversation continued between soulful bites and Marshall's exclamations of, "This is the best thing I've ever tasted!" My son has always loved macaroni and cheese, not realizing that it's part of his DNA structure to do so. I smiled to myself as I heard Miss Jackson and her sister encourage Marshall to eat up and eat plenty, just like I was always told. He was home now, and he did both. We continued to laugh and talk as the food took us to places too long forgotten and memories worth recalling.

Several hours later — and I am certain several pounds heavier — we were back in the car. We'd made an early start of the day, and it was barely one o'clock; there was still plenty of time to call on my older relatives living in Glen Allan before the day was through. Barbara reminded me that we had presents to buy for the folks in Glen Allan. But before we headed to Stein Mart to shop for gifts, I had to stop and visit my best friend from high school,

Henderson Fields, and his family. I followed the directions to Henderson's place that I'd written carefully on a note to myself. At the house, we all piled out of the minivan and walked across the grass to the kitchen door.

"Dad, don't walk on people's grass," chided Marshall behind me. "Why are you going to the back door? Haven't you learned anything living in Tulsa? I bet you didn't even call them. Mama, Daddy's been gone for years, but he's still Glen Allan."

Marshall kept it up all the way to the door. Finally, I had to tell him, "Son, we are visiting friends, not strangers."

People can solve any problem if they work together.

FRANKLIN D. ROOSEVELT

Seven

enderson's wife, Margaret, came to the door first, followed swiftly by my old high school friend himself. Soon we were all hugging and laughing and doing an on-the-spot check to see how well we were all holding up. Henderson's wavy black hair was going gray, but his football build was still in fine form. Margaret didn't look one day older. Her smile was just as it had been when we were students in school. Her dark skin still had that glow that made other women jealous and her husband proud. We were ushered into the family den where we were welcomed by their daughters, who were now almost grown, both of them attending college and working.

I hoped that Marshall noticed just how close we sat together; close enough so we could reach out and touch each other as we laughed over the memories that had woven our lives together as friends. This is the type of closeness I experienced in the small front rooms of my youth, where every heart was within reach. In Glen Allan, when I was growing up, the Christmas season brought everyone, young and old alike, together more closely than any other time of year. My older relatives and their friends would sit around the stove chewing tobacco and telling stories. The young ones, like me, would come close to watch and listen and learn. Our visiting was always done within arm's reach of each other.

Now that we were settled in with the Fields, Marshall had to repeat his plans for his life once more. We listened in turn as they told us about their children, where they were living, what they were doing. We were introduced to their daughter-in-law and told we would soon meet their older son. All the while, the cinnamon, spice, and nutmeg smells of holiday baking warmed the house. Telling old stories, our laughter seemed to dance across the shiny hardwood floor.

Margaret, a teacher, is also an excellent cook, and Henderson did not mince words praising her skills. He insisted that we taste everything she had baked for the holidays. I never would have guessed we could eat anything after the lunch we had just come from, but we happily loaded plates with slices of pie and cake, spoonfuls of yams with marshmallows, and baked vegetables layered with cheese. Barbara was delighted by several dishes and asked for the recipes. Marshall parked himself by the spinach dip and holiday punch and made himself at home, sampling various treats as they were offered. He seemed to be quietly enjoying the company of people he had never known, but with whom he felt completely at ease.

In the midst of our feast of laughter and good food, Henderson left the room. A few minutes later, he returned, pushing a wheelchair with his mother-in-law, Mrs. Johnson, in it. I listened as Margaret explained how they teamed up to take good care of her. I had known Mrs. Johnson well, and now I reminded her of the church song she always liked to sing, "Thank You, Sir," one of those soul-stirring hymns that make the wooden rafters shake and the congregation swing to the beat. I could still hear her voice rising up and filling the church with song. The words were simple: "Thank you, sir. I just want to stop and say thank you for all you've done." Her voice always brought new meaning and richness to those words as she closed her eyes and focused on her faith. She brightened and gave a coy laugh as we all acknowledged her gift of song.

Later, I saw ample evidence of how lovingly her family cared for her in her old age. While we were eating, I could see that feeding herself had become a difficult task. Once, as she was shakily bringing a bite of food to her mouth, it started to slide off the spoon. As if on signal, all of her children and grandchildren leaped out of their seats and scrambled to catch it before it could land on her bright white dress.

Later, as we hugged and said goodbye, Henderson, now Reverend Fields, laid his big football player's hands on Marshall's shoulders and personally challenged him to go out into the world and do good.

"Marshall, you look just like your father," said Henderson. "You know he was one smart guy in school. Couldn't play an ounce of sports, but was keen on the books. You'll do all right. You got it in you."

Marshall nodded as he shook Henderson's hand.

We had one more stop to make before we headed for Glen Allan, and that was a quick dash into Stein Mart to collect a few gifts for the folks at home. Barbara and I both remembered Stein Mart from our childhood. It was prominently located on the grand shopping street at that time, Washington Avenue. In our small-town world, Washington Avenue and Stein Mart were the big city. Barbara and I didn't know each other then, but both of our families shopped at Stein Mart for our school clothes and Sunday best. Marshall shook his head in utter disbelief as he listened to his mom and dad go on and on about a clothing store and the pains and joys of "colored" shopping. Greenville was segregated during our youth, and it affected almost every aspect of our lives. When we were growing up, even the dressing rooms in the department stores were segregated, which meant there weren't any for African-Americans. Our parents developed a keen ability to hold up a shirt or a pair of pants and judge which size would fit us. Now we almost laughed, thinking of how unnatural segregation was. Both the white store clerks and the "colored" shoppers had to work hard to maintain the walls of segregation, which were endlessly vulnerable to the greater human urge toward togetherness.

The Stein Mart parking lot was overflowing with cars and busy shoppers, but we were determined to get in and make our purchases. I didn't want to show up at home without presents for Aunt Girtha Mae, Cousin Sister, and Uncle Zee. As I angled for a parking spot, I was momentarily overcome with sadness. Our Christmas list was so short. When I was a kid, our list of relatives was very long. There were so many people I still wanted to give gifts, but the greater number of them were no longer with us. I would not be getting a gift for my great-grandparents or Ma Ponk, my aunt who raised me. Uncle Cleve was gone and so were Uncle Johnny and Cousin Beauty. They had all given me treasures in my growing-up years, pouring out their love in countless ways daily. I tried to remember their love and not think of them being gone.

It was already starting to get dark. There wasn't much time to shop if we were going to make it to Glen Allan at a reasonable hour. We rushed inside and raced through the old familiar store like people on a mission, grabbing scarves, warm slippers, and special cakes. I would have loved to pick up a tin of tobacco for Daddy Julius and an armful of bright wool wraps for my great aunts, who were always fighting off chills that could bring on the pleurisy. I stopped and stared at the holiday hubbub all around me in a daze, carried back again to those fond days of my childhood. Daddy Julius had been gone a long time, but I could still see him as plain as day. Marshall grabbed my arm and insisted we get a few boxes of fancy candy.

We added gift bags and candied fruits to our purchases of chocolates, slippers, warm hats, and knitted
scarves, and finally felt that no one had been overlooked.
Back in the car, we headed down Highway One to Glen
Allan. It was early evening and already the road was dark.
Barbara clicked on the cabin light and started counting
the money in our wallets. When I was a kid, money was a
luxury and people didn't have it everyday. At Christmas
time, however, small gifts of money magically appeared.
Now I wanted to continue that tradition for the people
who had done so much for me. Barbara divided up our
cash and tied it into little bundles with ribbon, then
slipped one into each of the gift bags. I watched her,
thinking of all the dear souls I missed. I thought of Aunt
Willie Mae and how she would have loved to fuss over
Marshall, and how one Christmas my Poppa Joe took me
to buy my first pair of pants that weren't blue jeans. I
thought about how my first grade teacher, Miss Mary
Maxey, would have questioned Marshall all about his
future, and how Poppa Joe, my great-grandfather, would
have stood on the front porch to welcome us. I said to
myself, "What a wonderful season to be loving and hurt-
ing at the same time!"

With the bright lights of Greenville slowly fading away
behind us, a sense of everything old and familiar came back
to me in the enveloping darkness. As I drove, I thought
about a similar trip I'd taken nearly thirty-five years earlier,
when I was Marshall's age and returning home.

I had left home in the summer of 1963 filled with the exhilaration and fear that comes with embarking on a voyage into the unknown for the first time. I was ready to go north and join the thousands of other black Southerners who had made a similar journey. Though I loved my family and all our friends, I was tired of picking cotton. I was ready to leave the fields behind. I was barely seventeen when I took the train north to St. Louis, where I knew I would find the freedom of integration, a change which hadn't yet reached our small Mississippi town. I was determined to get a good job and never pick or chop cotton again. My train ride to St. Louis was all that I imagined it would be. I was in awe of the porters and the scores of people getting on and off at each stop. Surely St. Louis would be everything I had dreamed.

Those first days in the big city were filled with excitement. I saw the tallest buildings I had ever seen. I could not stop talking about the three- and four-story town flats where black people actually lived. During that first weekend, I was invited to go with my new friends to an area in St. Louis called Gas Light Square. From their conversation, I could hardly wait to see this area where clubs and bars and intoxicating music filled the night. I would never have witnessed such a scene in Glen Allan. In many instances, inhibitions were thrown to the wind and our young dreams came true in those smoky clubs on the square. But as time passed and the brightness of the nightlife dimmed, I began to miss the people back home.

I began to miss their familiar voices. I was surrounded by people, but they were strangers. I never told anyone, but I was growing more and more homesick every day. Even though I worked downtown and caught the city bus to work, I still missed the conversations that had warmed my heart while I rode out to the fields to pick cotton on the back of Mr. Walter's truck. I had a job washing dishes in a large downtown department store; not the job of my dreams. Unable to keep up socially with many of my new city friends, I realized I was still a country boy at heart.

At that time, when I was first making my way out into the world, America was becoming increasingly embroiled in the Vietnam War. Young men my age were leaving daily and returning home in body bags. My draft number was relatively low and young black males were being called up every week. I was scared and alone in a big city that hardly knew my name, and I wondered if I would be next. Every day at work, the guys I worked with talked about who had died and who had been wounded. It seemed as if all the young black men were being sent to the front lines, and so many of them would never come home again. I told no one about my draft number. I kept my feelings to myself, trying to be a man in a world that was as strange to me as Vietnam itself. Even church was not the safe place I wanted it to be. On Sunday mornings, Elder Scott would read the names of the young men who had gone across the waters to serve America, but would not be coming home. I didn't want to be drafted and sent to Vietnam as an infantry soldier. Without consulting the few new adults in my life, I chose what I felt was my best option. I enlisted in the United States Air Force.

Within days, my world changed. Instead of washing dishes and riding the bus in St. Louis, I was on the Texas Lone Star train, packed together with hundreds of other young men headed to Lackland Air Force Base for basic training. At Lackland, marching daily under the hot Texas sun became my new way of life. The tedium of marching reminded me of trudging down the long rows of cotton, and my mind wandered back to Glen Allan. During the hours of marching, I had plenty of time to replay conversations with my great grandpa, my aunts and uncles, and all the people I had known. I began to understand the treasure I'd left behind.

My memories of their faith in me gave me the strength to get through basic training and technical school. After technical school, I had a month's leave before being assigned to Dow Air Force Base in Bangor, Maine. Maine was not the most coveted assignment among my fellow tech school grads, but it seemed like it just might be paradise compared to Vietnam. Bangor kept me from being sent directly to Vietnam. Still, it was common knowledge that young airmen with my classification stationed at Dow were eventually being shipped to Southeast Asia.

I figured that I was only postponing the inevitable, that within a few short months, I would surely be reassigned to the war zone. I wanted to go home one more time before then. With the prospect of Vietnam's jungles looming in my mind, I made plans to return to the place I had so desperately wanted to leave behind. I wanted to see Ma Ponk, and Poppa Joe, my great-grandfather, who had helped to raise me. I missed the community of relatives who had loved me and made a place in their lives for me when I was born to a teenaged mother. In St. Louis, I'd missed Ma Ponk's constant admonitions to make something of myself. She was determined that the circumstances of my birth would in no way impede my progress. She had taken over my rearing after Mama Pearl, my mother's grandmother, had died. I needed their blessings. I needed their challenge. I needed their voices to tell me that everything would be all right.

It was a long Greyhound ride home, but when it finally ended, my favorite uncle, Johnny, was at the bus station to pick me up. Greenville was still segregated, but I didn't care, Uncle Johnny was there with a smile as big as the grill on his car.

"Boy, stand up tall, lemme look at ya. You sho looks fine. That uniform fits you good."

I was taller and thinner, with my hair shaved off and a blue uniform that left plenty of room for me to grow, but Uncle Johnny looked me up and down and said I "sho" looked fine. I knew I was home.

The South I had left behind was changing fast. Uncle Johnny brought me up to date on the Civil Rights Movement and all the dangers that many of the participants faced, especially their friend Spike. Spike was one of the local Civil Rights leaders who had brought the Movement to Glen Allan. I listened quietly as he talked about the Ku Klux Klan while spitting tobacco juice out the car window.

"You know, Cliff, as I see it, God made us all and I can't understand why in the world we can't see that. Now all the white folk ain't bad, but those that is is making it mighty tough. We'll get through it. They can burn all the crosses they want. You know fire don't last forever."

I just listened as he told me about their war, and I weighed my thoughts about the war I anticipated.

When we got to Glen Allan, Uncle Johnny drove me directly to Ma Ponk's house. She was standing on her front porch, waiting and watching. I was expected. My heart swelled as I fell into her arms, smelling the Garrett snuff kisses I knew so well. After talking and putting away my clothes, I ran to visit my mother, who lived across the road. Next I walked down to see Daddy Julius and Miss Ida, then I walked down to Poppa's house. Poppa lived in a big, rambling place with a long front porch that always said welcome. He was out front with his ever-present pipe in hand.

"What do you think, Poppa?" I asked, as I made my way over to where he always stood, right by the door.

"Sissy, come on out here and see this boy. He looks good. The service is all right. Little light, but he looks good."

My step-great-grandmother came from the kitchen,

and for a moment, we all just stood and grinned. Poppa and I were always close, and even being all grown up in my Air Force uniform couldn't put any barrier between us. We hugged and hugged as he ushered me into the front room where we would sit and talk man to man. I didn't know that this would be the last time I would see my Poppa. He died not long after, while I was at Dow Air Force Base, and I was unable to get home in time for his funeral. That last visit and the image of him sitting in his worn, overstuffed chair in the front room are always with me.

Eight

liff. Cliff, don't miss your turn. Didn't you see the sign?"

Barbara knew me well enough to know where my thoughts were. I glanced back and chuckled to myself at Marshall in the back seat, sound asleep. Soon he'd be rubbing his eyes and asking, "Daddy, how much further do we have to go?" just like a kid.

We were getting close. What I couldn't see, I could feel. A few minutes later, I was able to make out the faint twinkle of lights emanating from Glen Allan in the distance. I felt a rush of tears. I always choked up when I got this close to home.

All along either side of the road were acres of barren land, but in my mind I could still see the rows of shotgun houses that used to be there. I heard the laughter of friends waiting to catch the school bus. I could smell Miss Bea Brown's homemade biscuits. These days, the Wildwood Plantation where we had all worked was just a

*Occasionally in life there are those moments of
unutterable fulfillment which cannot be completely explained
by those symbols called words. Their meanings can only
be articulated by the inaudible language of the heart.*

MARTIN LUTHER KING JR.

memory. Where was Pap? Where was Willie Reed? There was no way I could help Marshall and Barbara to see those vanished houses, and all the people who used to live in them, and the rows of cotton growing up in every direction. It was all gone.

We drove on past Lake Washington, which was gleaming with silver moonlight. The lakefront was where many of Glen Allan's white residents lived, and as we sped past, we caught glimpses of Christmas trees decked with lights through the front windows. When I was a kid, I'd had a job in this neighborhood, working for an elderly lady called Miss Knight, raking fig leaves from the orchard in her backyard. That house was gone now, torn down to make room for the Baptist church's parking lot. I tried to point out to Marshall, where I once worked, but even the fig trees were gone.

Glen Allan was not what it used to be, and I wanted to get past the vacant uptown quickly. At one time, the Christmas season in Glen Allan was a bustling, colorful affair. The streets would be filled with people from all of the small plantations around Glen Allan, coming to load up on groceries and get those small gifts that their children would cherish, some purchased on credit and some purchased with the hard-earned cash they'd tucked away throughout the year. Up and down the main street, friends and neighbors would greet each other with hearty slaps on the back and rousing cries of "Christmas gift!" the Glen Allan equivalent of "Merry Christmas."

I knew without looking that the Dixie Theater was gone, but I still remembered all the fun I'd had while sitting in the darkened cinderblock building watching the *Green Archer*. We all gathered at the movie theater, and when there was a new show in town everyone would be there. Back then, there was a thriving network of uptown groceries, dry goods stores, and restaurants owned by a diverse mix of ethnicities. There was Mr. Walter's café, Ty Quong's grocery, Mr. Hilton's supermarket, and Freid's Hardware. When I was growing up, the main street of Glen Allan was my Times Square. Now all of those businesses were boarded up.

I turned at the Black Methodist church, Allan Chapel AME, right across the street from the Harrisons' old grocery store. I'd been making this turn all my life, but the church had changed. I'd loved the Allan Chapel the way it used to look, a majestic old wooden building with a steeple that reached for the sky. It was gone, and in its place was a modern brick building. It was all right, I suppose, and sturdier, but it would never be as beautiful as Allan Chapel for me.

Christmas at the old Allan Chapel was celebrated with great fanfare. One night a year, the field hands and tractor drivers, maids and gardeners were splendidly transformed into Roman and Jewish citizens from biblical times for the reenactment of the nativity. The actors wrapped themselves in bright chenille bedspreads and wool blankets and witnessed the birth of Christ. The sound of the season was never better than when Uncle Hurley lent his baritone voice to a stirring rendition of "It Came upon a Midnight Clear." Though we were deep in the Mississippi Delta, the biblical Middle East came to Glen Allan every Christmas.

I drove past the place where the quarters — small two-room houses — used to be, the one place near uptown where "coloreds" had lived. Soon I could see Aunt Girtha Mae's car and bright lights coming from her front-room window. We had barely knocked when the door opened wide.

"Y'all come on in, Baby. Barbara, girl, you sho looks good, and look at Aunt Girt's big boy. What y'all feeding this boy?"

We all piled into the tiny front room, which was stuffed with evidence of all the living that Aunt Girtha and Uncle Johnny had managed through the years. Graduation pictures were everywhere, alongside wedding pictures, christenings, and reunions. Christmas decorations were wedged between ceramic figurines, lamps, and plush animals dragged back from outings to county fairs. Finding a place to sit, we settled down for the usual repertoire of inquiries about health and family. I asked Aunt Girtha how she was feeling, and felt a stab of sadness about my Uncle Johnny, who had passed away.

Though she was older now, her smile gave no hint of waning with age. After we had had a good talk and given her her gift bag stuffed with presents and good wishes, we stood to leave.

"Going to visit Sister next?" she asked.

"Yes'm," I replied as I had always done.

"Where to next, Mr. Taulbert?" came Marshall's voice from the back seat as we left Aunt Girt's house and drove down the once well-maintained street, now dotted with potholes.

"Just don't you worry," I said. "Wherever we go, you'll see, because you'll be with us."

"We are going to visit Cousin Sister," his mother said, as I tried to miss broken bottles, mud-filled potholes, and congregating young people I didn't know. There were few good ways to make a living in Glen Allan now that cotton farming was over, and even the roads showed the strain of a crippled local economy. At last, we pulled up to Cousin Sister's trailer; her original home had burned down many years earlier. I know that my family saw a small trailer with a screened-in porch built onto the front of it sitting on a bare, dimly lit lot, but I saw the warm, inviting house I used to know when Cousin Sister was raising her grandson, my cousin Bobby. We always visited Sister's house at Christmas as we made our way up the road to visit Aunt Big Dump and others. Her dining room table would be like a pastry shop, stacked with every kind of cake and pie imaginable. She was nearly one hundred years old now, and still living on her own.

I walked up and tapped at the screen door leading to the porch. It was locked, but I could see lights on in the house, so I kept knocking.

"Daddy, nobody's there," said Marshall, but I kept knocking until I heard a familiar voice call, "Who out there?" Sister was home.

"Sister, it's me, Cliff."

"Who?"

"It's me, Cliff, from Tulsa."

"Why didn't you say so? Lemme get to the door. I'm cooking."

We heard the sound of multiple latches being drawn and a chain being unhooked and at last the door opened, releasing a knee-weakening waft of freshly baked sweet potato pie. Adjusting her eyes to the darkness, our cousin made her way across the porch to meet us. She was a mere wisp of a woman with dark, chiseled features and glorious white hair, dressed in a terrycloth jogging suit. She looked up and flashed the smile that I remembered so fondly, the one I had wanted Marshall to see. That smile was the reason we were in Glen Allan.

"C'mon in this house, Boy, and you too, Barbara. You brought the boy this time, I see."

"Yes'm, I brought Marshall. He needed to come home."

"Course he did. Ain't nothing like home."

Though the trailer was small, Sister's hospitality was as big-hearted as it had always been. She made sure that we all had a comfortable place to sit, and before we could get our coats off, she offered us something good to eat. The little kitchen inside her trailer contained every delectable smell and flavor of Christmas there was. Nutmeg and cinnamon wiped away the odors of medicine and old age and pushed out the walls of the cramped rooms, so that Cousin Sister's tiny home grew to contain all the caring and joy of a long and fruitful life.

Not one to sit down and talk, she kept busy in the kitchen, walking back and forth and talking about how well her latest batch of pies were browning. I was amazed that, at her age, her diligent attention to Christmas baking had not changed. She had already sent a homemade potato pie to Uncle Zee.

"He had to have his Christmas from me," she said with a nod.

I laughed when she said that because I understood how, over the years, she had become mother and grandmother to all of us, and she took her role seriously. She was our spiritual watchtower and keeper of our lives.

Near the end of our visit, Marshall went out to the minivan and returned with our presents for Cousin Sister and Uncle Zee. Sister arranged the gifts carefully on the counter that separated the kitchen from the front room. She would attend to presents tomorrow. Today was Christmas Eve, the day for baking. Tomorrow was the day for opening presents.

As we made ready to leave, I looked at Sister's wrinkled, shining face and saw in her all the family I had known and loved for so many years. We had spent a full day going from house to house laughing, hugging, and being loved by people who made this time of year special by opening their hearts and homes. We walked out into the brisk night air with the warm smell of vanilla on our clothes and Cousin Sister's kisses on our faces. I looked at my son. He was holding an apple that Cousin Sister had given him. The long day of visiting was probably more than he bargained for, and I knew he was tired. It was late, and we still had to drive another hour to a family friend's home where we would stay and spend Christmas.

I sighed happily as I backed up and started down the road away from Cousin Sister's. Marshall had observed it all, shaken hands a dozen times, and given an account of himself at each gathering. I didn't want this time to end and this feeling to go away.

"Marshall, you have seen one of the rocks in our foundation. Cousin Sister was here when I was born. She was here when my mama was born. She has seen so many children grow up and go out into the world. She cares for us all."

"She's strong for such a small woman, Daddy," said Marshall. "I don't know if I could stay in that little trailer all alone."

"Well, son, she is living by herself, but she's not alone. Her son, Buddy, lives two streets over, and the people all around know that she is always up to visiting."

This time, Marshall didn't rush to plug his ears with music. He just sat up and looked at me in the rearview mirror. "I guess that's where you and grandma get it from," he said. "All that visiting and hugging. It's a Glen Allan 'thang.'"

Out of the corner of my eye I saw Barbara smile.

I nodded. "I know you wanted to go to Florida, Marshall. I know the guys probably had a great time, but I needed to give you a chance to meet some of these people before they're all gone. Your life has been so different from what mine was — and I am glad. But sometimes I worry that you didn't get enough of a sense of family and community in Tulsa. Life is different there. You didn't have a chance to feel the strong ties of an extended family the way I did. I wanted you to see that this is your family, too."

"Dad, don't worry. I understand the Glen Allan 'thang,'" he said, as he took the apple Cousin Sister gave him, rolled it up in a sweater on the seat and tucked it away.

I smiled to myself. "Yeah, I guess it is a Glen Allan 'thang,' son. I guess it is."

The first cold drops of a winter night storm hit the windshield as we drove back through the darkened main street of Glen Allan and onto the highway. We were leaving the vestiges of a place and a way of life that was quickly disappearing, one where relationships were tended daily like a vegetable garden in the hot Delta sun. Marshall's world was indeed vastly different from this — bigger, faster, and, in many ways, colder. It was defined by technology and the Internet, a new international conflict, constant strife in the

Middle East, and economic and political turmoil around the globe. Although his life was punctuated by a degree of indulgence and luxury unheard of in the rural South, it was also cut off from the strong ties and support that had always sustained me in challenging times.

Now more than ever, I wanted Marshall to know that something as simple as vanilla flavoring stirred into sweet potato pie was important, that visiting the older people was important, and that extending the definition of family to include all the people close to you was important. I had set out to show my son that family and friends are forever, and that reaching out to the ones you love, particularly in the holiday season, is always the right thing to do and the best way to celebrate. I felt certain that he would remember this trip throughout his life.

Whether he knew it or not, today his definition of the word "home" had changed.

*Don't be dismayed at good-byes. A farewell is necessary
before you can meet again. And meeting again, after moments
or lifetimes, is certain for those who are friends.*

RICHARD BACH

Reflections

*P*erhaps, having read about my journey with my family, you are reminded of your own hometown, your own journeys to the places where you got your start in life, and the people who gave you that start. Perhaps a long car trip has also given you a chance to talk with your family about your heritage. Here are some questions we might reflect on:

Can a trip to the places we remember from childhood be of value to our children who live in a vastly different world?

Can we draw strength from a journey that might remind us of unpleasant events?

Can we show our children our humanness while also showing them our trail to their lives and our future together?

By showing them all this, can we impress upon them the importance of building and sustaining good relationships throughout all the times of their lives?

How often do you go home?

Do you insist your children go with you?

Do you enjoy sharing the story of your life?

Do you schedule visits with the keepers of your history?

Do you enjoy the family foods that always made you smile?

Do you sit on the front porch in worn chairs and laugh out loud?

Do you cry with your family when you talk about loved ones no longer on the porch?

Do you stop by the small school you once attended and share the story of your favorite teacher?

Do you visit the church where you were known as somebody's son, grandson, daughter or niece?

Do you tell your children that their past is the foundation upon which their future will rest?

When will you make your journey home?

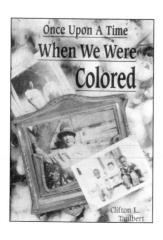